EMTs and Paramedics

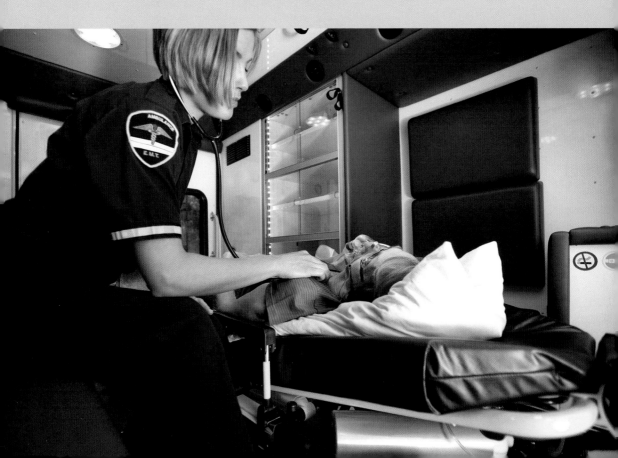

Careers in Healthcare

Athletic Trainers
Clinical & Medical Laboratory Scientists
Dental Hygienists
Dietitian Nutritionists
EMTs & Paramedics
Nurses
Occupational Therapists
Orthotists & Prosthetists
Physical Therapists
Physician Assistants
Respiratory Therapists
Speech Pathologists & Audiologists
Ultrasound Technicians

CAREERS IN
HEALTHCARE

EMTs and Paramedics

Samantha Simon

MASON CREST
PHILADELPHIA

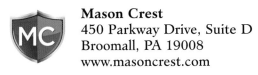

Mason Crest
450 Parkway Drive, Suite D
Broomall, PA 19008
www.masoncrest.com

©2018 by Mason Crest, an imprint of National Highlights, Inc.

Printed and bound in the United States of America.

CPSIA Compliance Information: Batch #CHC2017.
For further information, contact Mason Crest at 1-866-MCP-Book.

First printing
1 3 5 7 9 8 6 4 2

Library of Congress Cataloging-in-Publication Data

on file at the Library of Congress
ISBN: 978-1-4222-3799-1 (hc)
ISBN: 978-1-4222-7987-8 (ebook)

Careers in Healthcare series ISBN: 978-1-4222-3794-6

QR CODES AND LINKS TO THIRD-PARTY CONTENT

Table of Contents

KEY ICONS TO LOOK FOR:

Words to understand: These words with their easy-to-understand definitions will increase the reader's understanding of the text while building vocabulary skills.

Sidebars: This boxed material within the main text allows readers to build knowledge, gain insights, explore possibilities, and broaden their perspectives by weaving together additional information to provide realistic and holistic perspectives.

Educational Videos: Readers can view videos by scanning our QR codes, providing them with additional educational content to supplement the text. Examples include news coverage, moments in history, speeches, iconic sports moments and much more!

Text-dependent questions: These questions send the reader back to the text for more careful attention to the evidence presented there.

Research projects: Readers are pointed toward areas of further inquiry connected to each chapter. Suggestions are provided for projects that encourage deeper research and analysis.

Series glossary of key terms: This back-of-the book glossary contains terminology used throughout this series. Words found here increase the reader's ability to read and comprehend higher-level books and articles in this field.

Road accidents are one of the most common 911 calls for ambulances and EMTs.

 Words to Understand in This Chapter

CPR—cardiopulmonary resuscitation; a medical procedure in which compressions are performed to restart a person's heart and lungs and to get these organs functioning properly.

EMT—an emergency medical technician.

intravenous line (also known as an IV)—a line inserted into a major vein and used to administer medication.

paramedic—a highly trained and skilled EMT, one who can perform more medical procedures than someone with regular, or basic, EMT certification.

What Do EMTs Do?

Throughout a person's life, anything can happen, including medical emergencies. The first responders to these medical emergencies are *EMTs*, emergency medical technicians, or paramedics. An EMT cares for and treats sick or injured people in emergency situations and settings.

On a normal call, 911 operators send an ambulance to the scene of the incident with two to four EMTs or *paramedics*, depending on the gravity of the emergency. Upon arrival, EMTs work hand and hand with police officers and firefighters to treat and help everyone who is injured at the scene. These scenes can range from a house fire to an automobile accident.

Not only do EMTs respond and offer treatment in emergency situations, they also transport patients from the site of an emergency to the proper medical facilities. This is done either by ambulance or by helicopter.

EMTs are considered entry-level patient care providers. They are formally known as EMT-1s or EMT-Bs (that is, basic EMTs). Many civilians believe that paramedics and EMTs are interchangeable, but paramedics undergo more intensive training and are able to perform more advanced lifesaving techniques. Some EMTs go on to become paramedics, firefighters, physician assistants, or doctors.

EMTs must be in good physical shape. Most EMT courses require students to pass a weight-lifting test proving that they can lift at least 125 pounds (57 kg).

Responsibilities of EMTs

EMTs and paramedics treat approximately 25 to 30 million people in the United States each year. They are responsible for the following:

- To respond to 911 calls for emergency medical assistance
- To assess a patient's condition and determine a course of treatment
- To provide first-aid treatment or life-support care to sick or injured patients
- To transport patients safely in an ambulance or helicopter to a medical facility
- To report their observations and treatment to physicians, nurses, or other health care staff upon arrival at a health care facility

All of the responsibilities listed above must be carried out in an effective and orderly manner. Most of the time ambulances carry two

Controlling Emotional Responses

An EMT who works with the ambulance service for a major hospital was asked to talk about experiences he had with traumatic events in which he had to separate himself from the emotions, such as losing a patient or tending to a very sick child. He was also asked for advice he would give to new EMTs on how to deal with this aspect of the job? He responded:

> "I am fortunate enough never to have lost a patient. I have tended to terminally ill patients. For any of these situations you must remember that you have one job and that is to safely transport the patients and help keep them stable until they reach their destination. If they are ill or they pass en route, you have to follow your protocols. When that call is done, you have to remember that there are more patients waiting for you and you cannot be emotionally distraught when you're treating them. You always have to have a clear head for your next patients, because you never know what is going to come your way down the road."

Transportation of patients can happen in an ambulance, in the air or sea.

to four EMTs. While one EMT is driving the ambulance, another will be administering treatment to the patient in the back. Similar procedures are followed in other different forms of emergency transportation, including in a helicopter or an airplane transporting patients.

When a 911 call comes in, the usual protocol for basic EMTs is as follows: First they get to the scene of the accident or incident in a timely and safe manner, avoiding any motor vehicle accidents on the way. On arrival, they "size up" the scene: This means that the EMTs determine what type of

Educational Video

To peek at a day in the life of an EMT, scan here.

incident occurred, whether the scene is safe, who is injured, how many people are injured, and whether additional help is necessary. Once this analysis of the situation is complete, they can start to work with the patients.

In responding to the scene of the accident, the first priorities for EMTs treating the injured include opening and maintaining a proper airway, ventilating patients, and administering *CPR*, or cardiopulmonary resuscitation, if necessary. Once those priorities are addressed, EMTs stop any bleeding, bandage any wounds, immobilize any broken limbs, and stabilize the patients' neck and spine. With that work complete, EMTs

There is always constant communication and documenting to allow for continuation of care for other medical professionals.

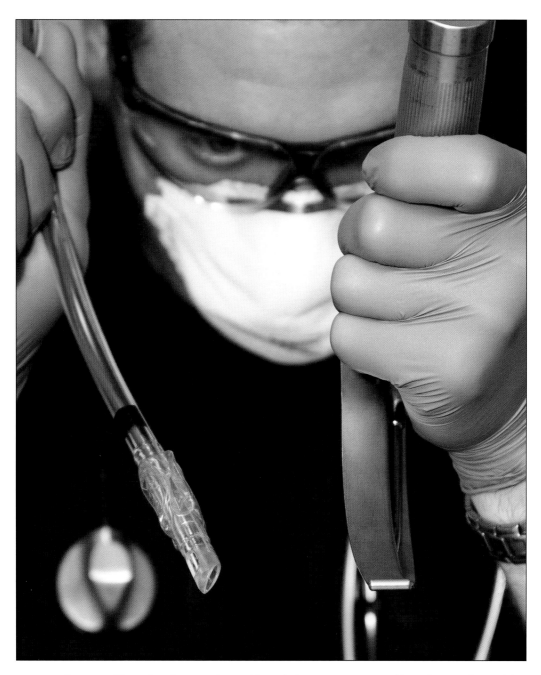

Paramedics are able to intubate patients, if needed. EMTs are not allowed to perform this procedure.

make sure patients are properly secured and harnessed, and transport them to the nearest medical facility. While doing all this medical work, EMTs also try to determine patients' medical history, identification information, and accident history so they can provide critical information for other emergency and medical personnel who treat the patient upon arrival at the medical facility.

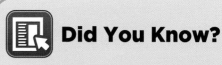

Did You Know?

According to the US Department of Labor's Bureau of Labor Statistics, over the past ten years, 58,000 EMTs and paramedics have changed their employment status, either moving to other health care jobs or leaving the field entirely.

As patients are en route to a medical facility, EMTs must be provide constant care, including assessing their patients' medical status on a minute-by-minute basis and adjusting their medical treatment accordingly. These decisions must also be documented and communicated clearly to the medical facility where the patients will receive further care.

Differences between EMTs and Paramedics

The acronym EMT stands for "emergency medical technician." The word paramedic has a Latin root, with para meaning "beside or beyond" and medic meaning "doctor or medicine." These two words are used interchangeably to describe an EMT. But a paramedic is the highest certified prehospital health care worker; paramedics can provide services that EMTs cannot.

An EMT can deliver patient care, like providing oxygen or treating a simple asthma attack or an allergic reaction; howev-

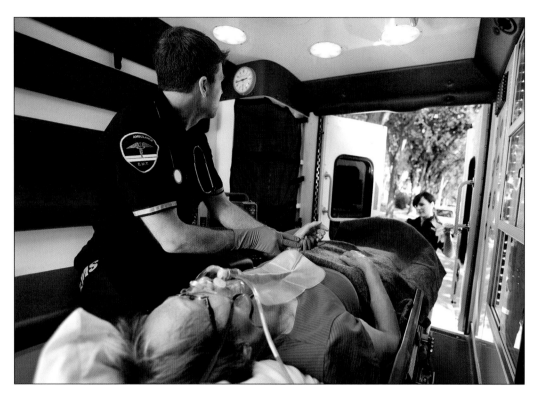

When transporting a patient in an ambulance, one EMT or paramedic may drive the ambulance while another monitors the patient's vital signs and gives additional care.

er, EMTs cannot break the skin of a patient, meaning they cannot give injections, except for certain cases where autoinjectors are needed to address life-threatening allergic reactions. Paramedics can perform procedures that go beyond breaking the skin of a patient, such as administering *intravenous lines*, starting chest tubes, doing EKG monitoring, and giving other lifesaving medical attention. Paramedics provide life support to patients that is similar to the care they receive in a hospital emergency room. Once licensed, paramedics can work in many different environments and deal with various people every day.

An EMT undergoes 120 to 150 hours of training in an EMT course. By contrast, a paramedic completes 1,300 hours of EMT training, plus more extensive academic training as well, often requiring much more time in classes and internships than EMTs to become certified. While both professions work hand in hand, paramedics have a greater knowledge of anatomy, cardiology, physiology, medications, and different emergency medical procedures than EMTs do.

 Text-Dependent Questions

1. What does the acronym EMT stand for?
2. Do the terms EMT and paramedic refer to the same jobs?
3. Can paramedics and EMTs perform the same procedures?

 Research Project

Check out the local ambulance programs in your community, both public and private. Find out the number of staff members they have—both paid and volunteer—as well as the kinds of emergencies they have responded to in the past year. Speak to the head of the ambulance corps and ask how they recruit and train their members.

EMTs and paramedics take their experience and training, and use it to move into other medical professions like physicians, nurses, and even laboratory scientists.

 Words to Understand in This Chapter

blood-borne illnesses—diseases or viruses that live in and are transmitted by blood.

continuation of care—the quality of care over time given to a patient by a medical team.

first responders—the initial personnel who rush to the scene of an accident or an emergency.

natural disaster—a disaster caused by weather or another nonhuman event.

A Look at the Opportunities

EMT training gives you a good grounding if you want to move up in the medical field. A lot of medical professionals start out as basic EMTs. As a *first responder*, you gain great experience that's valuable in a variety of different medical professions. For example, many EMTs choose to become nurses, physician assistants, laboratory technicians, and even doctors.

In addition to venturing into other medical professions, EMTs can grow within the first responder field. A basic EMT can take a course to become an advanced emergency medical technician. Advanced emergency medical technicians can do everything that basic EMTs can do, but they can also perform some of the procedures that paramedics can. An advanced EMT is an intermediate level between a basic EMT and a para-

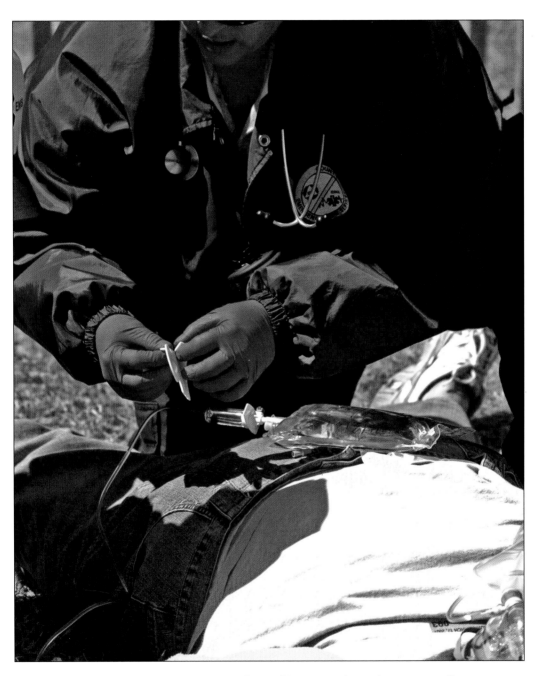

Both EMTs and paramedics are constantly working on patients, but paramedics are usually the ones putting in IV lines.

medic. An EMT can also become a paramedic or even a trained firefighter and a paramedic.

Many EMTs also choose to become volunteers, working for rural or small-town ambulance corps and EMT units, or for national relief organizations. Also, not all EMTs are affiliated with ambulance corps, fire departments, or hospitals. Some EMTs work for private hotels, casinos, theme parks, or other facilities.

EMTs and paramedics work in many different environments, including large theme parks, hotels, and even cruise lines. EMTs working in venues like these are usually there to

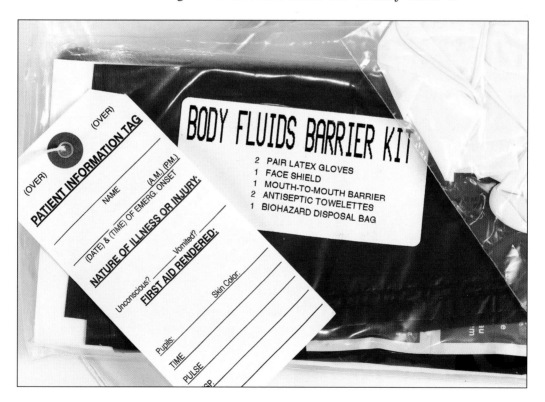

On a daily basis, EMTs and paramedics are in constant close contact with patients and their bodily fluids.

Did You Know?

No two days in an EMT's professional life are ever the same. The number of dispatch calls varies every day, and each day you go out on different kinds of calls, meaning you never know what can happen on the job from one minute to the next.

provide first aid to guests at these travel destinations and lodgings. These EMTs help guests with emergency medical situations, offering basic medical assistance and *continuation of care* if the guest needs to be transported to a medical facility off site. Usually, these EMTs only perform very basic medical procedures and administer very basic medications, even if they are higher-trained EMTs or paramedics; this is for the safety of the guests and so the theme parks and hotels avoid liability.

To work on a cruise ship, however, an EMT must be a certified paramedic and have a minimum of two years of paramedic experience and current professional certifications. These cruise-line paramedics are usually the first line of medical care aboard the cruise ship. They respond to emergency situations, treat sick and injured passengers, and work with the rest of the medical team on the cruise ship in providing continuation of care.

Educational Video

To see a short video on ten things people should know about EMTs, scan here.

Another factor EMTs and paramedics must take into account is their physical condition and their health status.

EMT Shifts, Explained

EMT shifts are much different from those in the corporate world. A professional was asked to explain the shifts EMTs work, and talk about the toll these can take on the person's health. He explained:

"EMT shifts vary, depending on where you work. When you work for a fire department, you will generally work 24 to 48 hours and then have a few days off. When you work for a private company, the hours vary from 8 to 24 hours per shift. These shifts can be as easy as zero calls to as many as one call an hour.

"For each call, you are lifting equipment and patients, maneuvering through all kinds of terrain, driving, reaching, and walking. Being an EMT is very demanding on the body. If the proper lifting techniques are not used, you can severely injure yourself. One of the keys to not injuring yourself or your patient is to make sure you get enough rest, eat healthy foods, stay hydrated, and exercise. With all of these components, you can ready your body to endure the demands of the job.

"For private ambulance agencies, you can choose an on-call shift. This means that they can call you at any time during your shift and you have to arrive at the station within an hour and be ready. They are on call for disasters or major emergencies. Some agencies have a disaster response team whose members are called in to work several days in a row without stopping until the disaster is over and everyone is medically taken care of."

According to the US Department of Labor, 48 percent of paid EMTs and paramedics work for ambulance services. Hospitals employ 16 percent of EMTs and paramedics, while fire departments and other government agencies employ 29 percent.

EMTs and paramedics are in constant motion, whether it is bending and kneeling, lifting, or moving patients. These movements require a lot of physical strength, stamina, and endurance, which means EMTs and paramedics must always be

knowledgeable about proper lifting and moving procedures, so they can keep both themselves and their patients safe and secure. This also puts EMTs and paramedics in very close prox-

Floods and other natural disasters can happen at any point, that is why EMTs and first responders must be ready for any emergency.

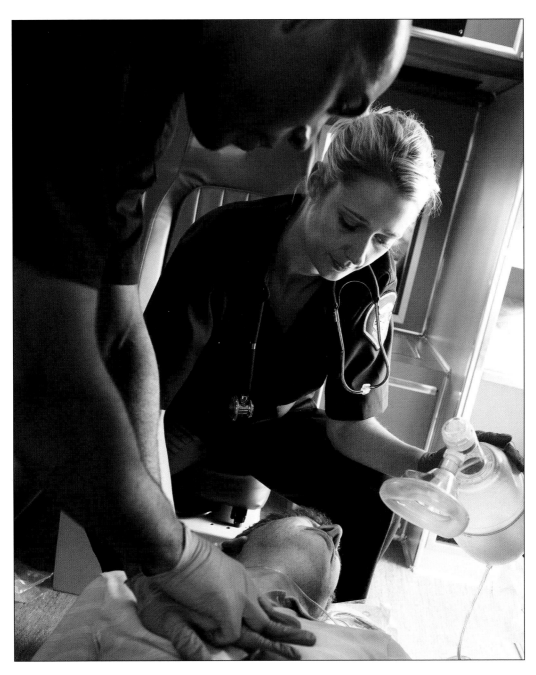

EMTs have the basic knowledge and skills necessary to stabilize and safely transport patients, using the basic equipment typically found on an ambulance.

imity to patients, which can expose these emergency medical personnel to contagious diseases, such as viruses and *blood-borne* illnesses like HIV.

According to the Bureau of Labor Statistics, employment of EMTs and paramedics is projected to grow by 24 percent from 2014 to 2024. This increase in demand for EMTs stems from the growing rates of chronic disease in the United States and the surging elderly population. There is also a huge demand for EMTs in rural areas and to respond to emergencies brought on by *natural disasters*.

 Text-Dependent Questions

1. True or False: At theme parks, EMTs can only administer basic first aid.
2. What is the percentage of job growth projected for EMTs and paramedics from 2014 to 2024?
3. Do EMTs work in close proximity to patients and bodily fluids?

 Research Project

Research theme parks or a cruise line in your state or region and find out if they hire EMTs or paramedics.

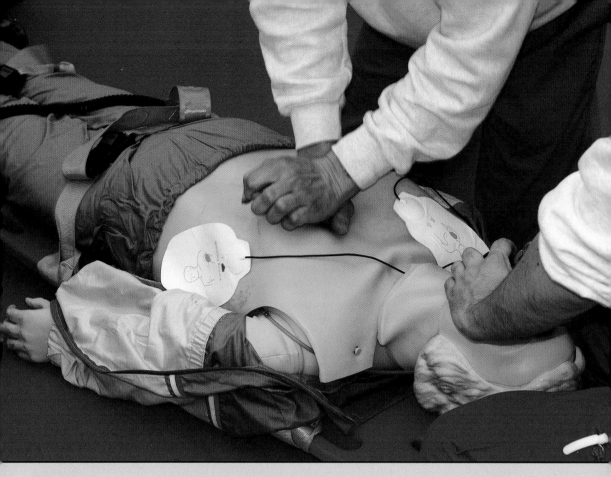

CPR certifications are a basic necessity for all students wanting to pursue any EMT training.

 Words to Understand in This Chapter

cardiac assessments—physical health assessments focusing on a patient's cardiac state, including the heart rate, electrical activity measured by an EKG, and any changes in heart function.

EKG—electrocardiogram; a test that measures the electrical activity of the heart.

EKG interpretation—an analysis of the electrical activity of the heart, based on the EKG.

interpersonal skills—communication and social skills that smooth the way between teams and among people working on teams.

Education and Training

I f you want to pursue a career as an emergency medical technician or a paramedic, your education and training must start in high school. The first step on the path to becoming an EMT is figure out if you want to get into the medical field. One way to determine whether a medical career is for you is by shadowing medical professionals while you're in high school or volunteering at a free clinic in your community. From this experience, you can gain firsthand experience in a medical environment. In addition to that, some high schools around the nation offer basic EMT courses on site.

Important Characteristics of EMTs

Even with the proper training and education, future EMTs should possess certain key traits to pursue a career in the emergency medical field. These include the following:

Compassion: EMTs and paramedics must be able to provide emotional support to patients during an emergency, especially those who are in life-threatening situations or extreme mental distress.

Interpersonal skills: EMTs and paramedics usually work in teams and must be able to coordinate their activities with others in very stressful situations.

Listening: Listening to patients and their fellow team members is a must for EMTs and paramedics. Listening enables them to determine the extent of the injuries or illnesses they're facing and the best way to handle those situations.

Physical strength: EMTs and paramedics need to be strong and physically fit; it is usually a requirement for these emergency medical personnel to lift 125 pounds (57 kg) or more.

Problem-solving: EMTs and paramedics must evaluate patients' symptoms, administer appropriate treatments, and solve the problems they confront quickly and efficiently.

Communication skills: Communicating clearly is crucial for EMTs and paramedics so they can explain procedures to patients and their team members, give orders, and relay information to others.

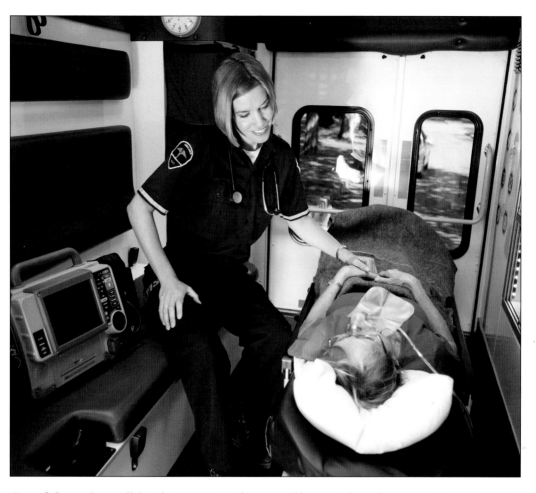

One of the main qualities that EMTs and paramedics must have is compassion, especially for their patients and their patients' families.

After receiving a high school diploma, along with cardiopulmonary resuscitation (CPR) certification, future EMTs are required to take and pass a rigorous training program before they can do this job in the field. These EMT programs are nondegree programs and fall into two categories—diploma programs or certificate programs. These types of programs are usually offered at community colleges, technical institutes, and other specialized education centers. In addition, many community colleges offer associate's degrees in the EMT-paramedic field.

EMT-B Diploma Programs

A diploma program gives graduates an Emergency Medical Technician-Basic (EMT-B) diploma. This diploma confirms that the holder has basic emergency medical skills and patient

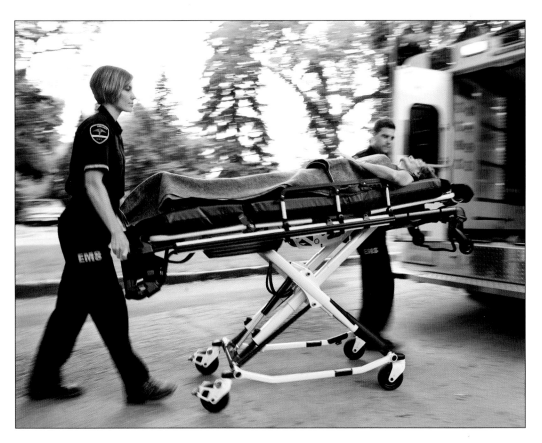

EMTs and paramedics must be in good physical shape to be able move and transport patients from accident sites.

assessment skills. To earn an EMT-B diploma, candidates must complete about 120 to 150 hours of education in medical procedure and working with basic medical equipment. The candidate must also do an internship, where, as an EMT-in-training, he or she will gain clinical experience assisting an ambulance crew or an emergency room staff.

 Did You Know?

A person holding an EMT-B certification can assess a patient's condition and manage respiratory, cardiac, and trauma emergencies. EMT-Bs usually ride with more highly trained EMTs and paramedics.

EMT Certificate Programs

EMT certificate programs are for a student who wants to become a basic, intermediate, or EMT- paramedic. The certificate program is more rigorous than the diploma program; it

 An EMT Talks About Training

A working EMT was asked to talk about the schooling and hands-on training he needed to become certified. He explained:

"To become an EMT you can take an accelerated course, which is four months long. This schooling includes terminology, basic anatomy, physiology, and hands-on basic life-support skills. My school required us to put in 36 clinical hours in a hospital and 90 hours on an ambulance."

combines more intensive and extensive classroom study and clinical practice. Certificate programs are usually divided into three levels: basic, intermediate, and paramedic. As you go from basic to intermediate to paramedic training, you spend more time in class, learning more about anatomy, physiology, cardiology, medical terminology, and *EKG interpretation*. In addition to in-class hours, these certificate programs also require you to do ride-along internships, which call for you to join and assist local ambulance corps or fire departments as their mem-

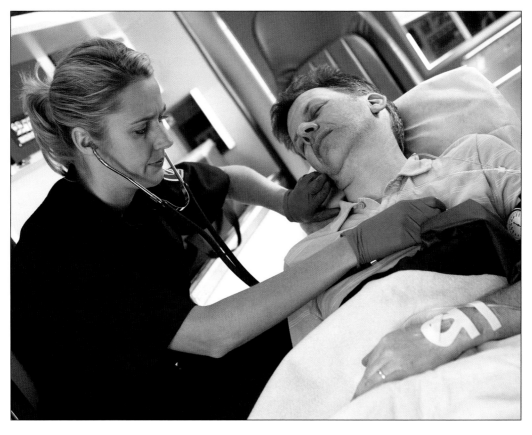

One of the main goals of an EMT is to stabilize the patient, and get the patient safely to the hospital.

Many EMTs and paramedics grow in their education and training to work for local fire departments and police departments.

bers respond to emergencies. Most certificate programs require upwards of 1,000 hours of schooling and training for an EMT-intermediate, and roughly 1,300 hours of schooling and training for an EMT-paramedic.

EMT Associate's Degrees

You may also obtain an associate's degree in the EMT-paramedic field. Most EMT associate's degree programs prepare students for EMT-paramedic licensure. This is a much more advanced and science-based curriculum than diploma or certificate programs. The curriculum for an associate's degree

Educational Video

Scan here for a short video on the medical assessment an EMT makes.

includes both general education courses, such as writing composition, and medical courses, such as anatomy and physiology, biology, lab courses, and classes specific to the theory and practice of medicine for emergency responders. Additionally, students acquire high-level EMT skills through extensive coursework, field experience, and clinical experience. In these associate's degree programs students learn skills in pharmacology, emergency trauma care, *cardiac assessment*, shock treatments, and patient management. These programs also require a longer internship time with a local ambulance corps or fire department than diploma or certificate programs do. It usually takes a full two years to complete an associate's degree program.

Licensing and Certificates

After completing one of these diploma, certificate, or associate's degree programs, EMTs are required to pass a licensing exam at either the national or the state level. This depends on the state where the EMT lives. The National Registry of Emergency Medical Technicians (NREMT) also offers a national certification exam. This certification exam contains both a multiple choice and a free-response portion. In most states, if you are licensed nationally by NREMT you are qualified in that state to perform the duties of a EMT. To apply for a national license with NREMT, you must be eighteen years of age and have completed an EMT course. Some states also require a background check before issuing their licensing and certifications, and prohibit applicants who have any criminal history from applying for an EMT license.

 Text-Dependent Questions

1. What are the two requirements to apply for national licensing with NREMT?
2. What certifications can a high school student earn in anticipation of pursuing a career as an EMT?
3. True or False: There are two portions to the licensing exam given by the National Registry of Emergency Medical Technicians—free response and multiple choice.

 Research Project

Research local colleges or universities in your area that offer EMT-paramedic programs. Learn how long these programs take to complete, how much they cost, and what type of diploma or certification you earn at the end.

An Union Army ambulance crew removes wounded soldiers from a battlefield during the Civil War.

 Words to Understand in This Chapter

ambulance-wagon—one of the first transportation ambulances; developed and used during the Civil War era.

prehospital setting—any setting where an accident or emergency takes place, and the route taken to the medical facility.

standardization—the practice of making things uniform, or similar in quality.

zone of combat—a war zone; an area of battle.

4

The Evolution of EMTs

Emergency medical services in America goes back as far as the Civil War era (1861–1865). All military personnel had to be examined by medical officers to qualify for duty; these were thought of as the original emergency medical services personnel. Trained doctors and staff usually set up usually set up an operating area roughly a hundred yards (about 91 m) from battle and typically flew a red flag above their tent so they could be easily identified by soldiers.

After the First Battle of Bull Run in July 1861, many appointed stretcher bearers fled from the battlefields and left the wounded stranded for days on end. The wounded soldiers who could walk made the 27-mile (43.5-km) journey back to Washington, D.C., to seek medical aid, and were often attended to in the capital by physicians who had never operated on

Many of the original EMTs and paramedics were trained during wartime.

patients before. In response to this horrific scenario, William A. Hammond, surgeon general of the US Army, made a series of changes in the procedures used to care for injured and wounded soldiers.

The greatest of Hammond's changes involved the transportation of the wounded, which became the responsibility of a newly formed army medical corps. Hammond then designed a superior *ambulance-wagon*, the first of its kind specifically built and equipped so that medical personnel could care for and treat wounded soldiers. Additionally, ambulances were assigned to each regiment. There was one ambulance for every

150 soldiers and two medical supply wagons for each regimental corps. Each ambulance team had personnel trained in patient care, and specially trained in caring for soldiers wounded on the battlefield.

In 1865, the first civilian ambulance, based on Hammond's design, was put into service in Cincinnati, Ohio. Other cities soon followed suit. But even as civilian ambulance services grew, most emergency medicine continued to be practiced in wartime situations.

During World War I, injured soldiers used flags and other signals to alert medical teams to their whereabouts on the bat-

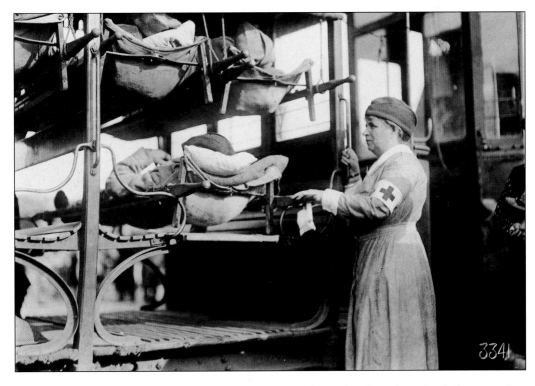

An American Red Cross nurse tends to wounded soldiers that have been loaded onto train cars in France, July 1918.

American medics load a dying civilian into an ambulance during World War II.

tlefield. These medical teams, primarily made up soldiers, also relied on other types of emerging technology, including electric-, steam-, and gasoline-powered carriages used for transporting the injured to local hospitals in war-torn places. These replaced horse-drawn vehicles.

Emergency and wartime medicine took a big leap forward during World War I. It was the first war to utilize traction splints to aid in immobilizing leg fractures; these substantially reduced battlefield deaths, compared to the older methods of amputation in the field. This use of new and improved medical technology prompted changes in civilian emergency medicine. After the war, civilian ambulances carrying surgeons were equipped with radio dispatchers, to better serve the community, and with traction splints to give patients a better chance of survival.

The evolution of the EMT-paramedic career started in earnest in the early 1970s, but its origins can be traced to 1966. That year, President Lyndon B. Johnson received a report on accidental deaths and disabilities in the United States at the time. This report, titled "Accidental Death and Disability: The Neglected Disease of Modern Society," stated that in 1965 motor vehicle accidents had killed more than 107,000 Americans, and disabled or permanently impaired more than 10 million more. Additionally, the report evaluated the care people were getting in an emergency, before they arrived at the hospital, and it showed that "if seriously wounded, chances of survival would be better in the *zone of combat* than on the average city street." The report even asserted that accidental injuries were the leading cause of death in an American's first half of life. This report then made sev-

In 1960 Senator John F. Kennedy, at the time a candidate for president, declared, "Traffic accidents constitute one of the greatest—perhaps the greatest—of the nation's public health problems."

Before the development of emergency medicine in the 1960s and 1970s, people were routinely transported to hospitals from accident scenes in modified vehicles that were similar to the hearses used by funeral homes.

eral recommendations for the *standardization* of ambulance design, emergency procedures, management of injuries in accidents, and training for all emergency personnel. These standards led to the first curriculum for a basic EMT. This is considered to be the document that launched the development of the modern EMT.

By 1972, interest in emergency medicine and emergency medical training was growing exponentially. Yet few people knew very much about emergency medicine. So, that year the University of Cincinnati established the first residency program to train people specifically in the practice of emergency medicine. In the same

Educational Video

To see a ride-along with an EMT on an emergency call, scan here.

program, nurses and physicians trained paramedics and EMTs in *prehospital settings.*

To become more standardized, the first board of what is now the National Registry of Emergency Medical Technicians (NREMT) was established in 1970. That same year, the board created a national certifying exam for all EMTs. In 1971, NREMT hired its first executive director and the first NREMT-ambulance exam was offered and taken by 1,520 people. Seven years later, in 1978, the first NREMT-paramedic exam was given in Minneapolis. That same year NREMT became a member of the National Commission for Health

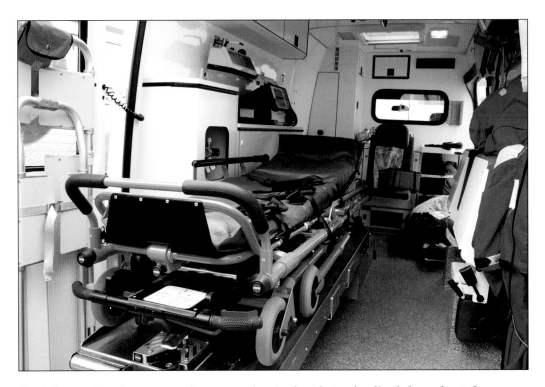

Ambulances have become much more modernized and standardized throughout the country.

Certifying Agencies. This also led to EMT-P (EMT-paramedic) becoming an approved health occupation through the Council of Allied Health Education and Accreditation (CAHEA).

From the 1970s to now, the EMT and paramedic curriculums have constantly been changing and evolving, with more standardizations and advancements in these curriculums. These changes have come about as a result of increasing education of emergency medical personnel. Also, the EMT has become an integral part of the health care team. Now there are well-established and excellent training programs all across the country for EMTs and paramedics, and these programs continue to focus on research into and development of the education of emergency and prehospital medicine.

Ambulances have also been standardized and now must meet national standards. Every ambulance in the United States

 EMT Technology Today

An EMT at a major hospital was asked to describe what sort of technology he used in doing his job each day. He responded:

"On an average day an EMT will use a stretcher, a blood pressure cuff, a pulse oximeter, and an accident-check machine. When EMTs are working with a paramedic, they will also help run an EKG machine—both 4 and 12 leads. On certain calls, an EMT may have to use oxygen, suction devices, oral and nasal airway devices, splints, and different backboards."

must now have particular lifesaving equipment and certain types of emergency equipment. This is mostly due to the work of organizations like NREMT, which helped develop and help establish these standards. NREMT is playing a major role on national medical committees and in the growing medical field.

 Text-Dependent Questions

1. From the 1970s to now, what has become standardized in the EMT world?
2. What is the major organization helping to set standards for ambulances and EMT training in the United States?
3. Where was the first NREMT-paramedic exam given in 1978?

 Research Project

Research the different emergency medical equipment carried in ambulances from the time of the Civil War until now—both civilian and military.

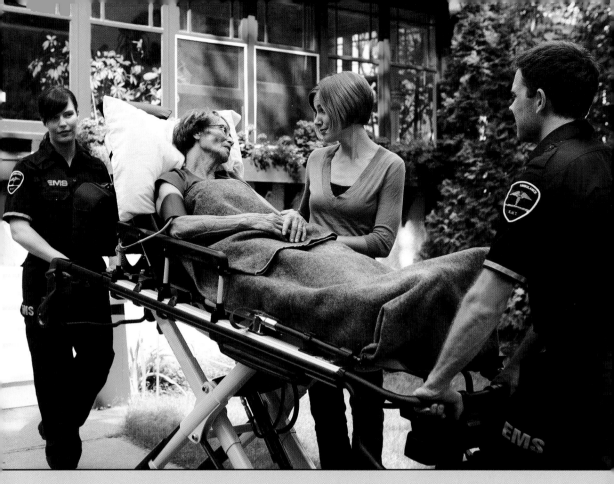

While training for their profession, EMTs and paramedics spend many hours working in the field, receiving hands-on training in addition to their classroom education.

 Words to Understand in This Chapter

dialysis—the process of removing waste products and excess fluid from the body. Dialysis is necessary when the kidneys are not able to adequately filter the blood.

field training—education gained on the job.

5

Overview and Interview

The National Emergency Number Association estimates that 240 million calls are made to 911 in the United States each year. With this enormous number of emergency calls coming in every year, emergency medical personnel are constantly needed. According to the Bureau of Labor Statistics, employment of EMTs and paramedics is projected to grow 24 percent from the years 2014 to 2024—a higher rate of growth than any other occupation in the United States.

The duties of an EMT include assessing a patient's condition and determining a course of treatment, providing first-aid treatment or life-support care to sick or injured patients, and transporting patients safely in an ambulance or helicopter to the proper medical facility. EMTs must also report their obser-

Educational Video

Scan here to see a video that details a day in the life of emergency service personnel.

vations and treatments on the scene and en route for physicians, nurses, or other health care staff on arrival to the medical facility to allow for continuation of care.

Every EMT must complete at least a basic EMT course. This could be a certification course or diploma course. One of these courses must be com-

Due to the millions of 911 calls received each year, EMTs and paramedics are always on the move.

Medical professionals working in hospital settings often help teach paramedic or EMT courses to help improve prehospital care.

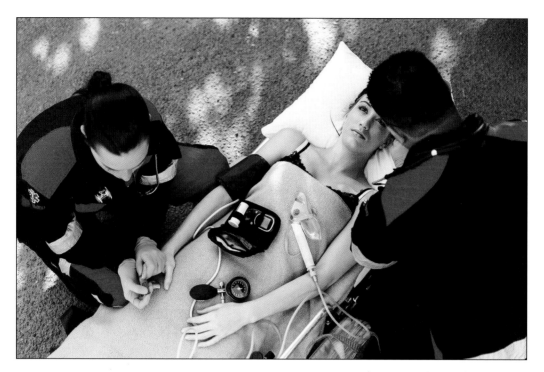

EMTs and paramedics are always working on teams to stabilize and transport the patients, so communication and teamwork are crucial.

pleted and a licensing exam must be passed. These courses have a mix of both classroom education and *field training* in emergency medical technique. This licensing exam can be either a national exam, such as that given by the National Registry of Emergency Medical Technicians (NREMT) or a state exam. In addition to the licensing, EMTs may also have to go through a criminal background check to prove they have no criminal record before they can work in the field.

In addition to their schooling, EMTs should also have the following traits: compassion, interpersonal skills, listening, physical strength, problem-solving, and finally communication skills. These skills are used on a daily basis and this is what makes EMTs and other emergency medical professionals so different from other medical professionals in the health field. EMTs and paramedics are the first medical personnel to arrive on the scene to an accident. They are also the first people to comfort, diagnose, and start any lifesaving procedures on the patient. Not only that, EMTs must be able to think quickly and work together. Because with every 911 call, there is no really no warning of what the EMT and paramedic team is about to encounter. No two emergency calls are the same. Another great

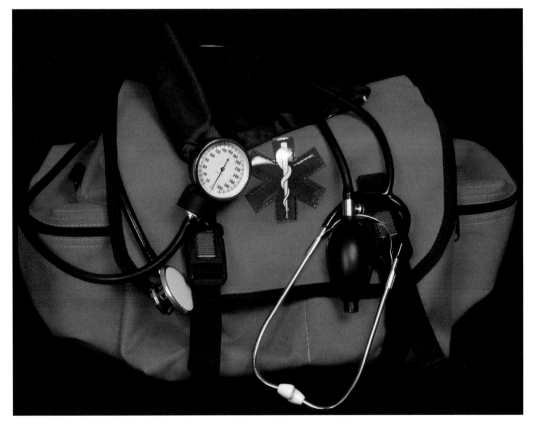

EMT and paramedics bring standardized equipment on each emergency call.

aspect of the EMT job is EMTs and paramedics can work in various places. They do not just have to work with an ambulance or with a hospital. EMTs find employment at theme parks or hotels and paramedics can work for a cruise lines. EMTs and paramedics also able to grow in their medical careers. A large amount of pre-medical and pre-physician assistant students get their clinical hours as EMTs and paramedics. EMT is a great profession for anyone wanting to gain a broad amount of medical anatomy, physiology, and emergency medical techniques that can be used in various other medical professions.

NREMT has worked hard to shape and mold the world of EMTs and paramedics to make these fields more standardized and respected medical professions.

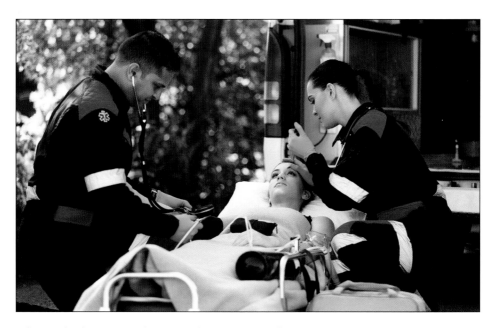

The work of EMTs and paramedics is physically strenuous and can be stressful, sometimes involving life-or-death situations.

Q&A with a Professional in the Field

What follows is the transcript of a firsthand interview from Ian Kramer, an EMT who is working in the field today. He works for AMR Medics Ambulance Service in Broward County Florida.

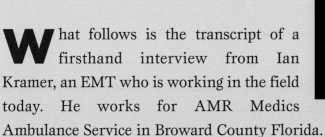

QUESTION: How long have you been an EMT?

Ian: "Four months."

QUESTION: What inspired you to get into this field?

Ian: "I am planning on going to school to become a physician assistant. To get into PA school you need clinical hours and patient care experience. Being an EMT is one of the best ways to gain that needed experience."

QUESTION: What types of classes do you take? What kind of hands-on training are you required to complete?

Ian: "I obtained my EMT schooling at a private school that had all of the classes in one course. If you attend a college to become an EMT, there are three different courses you have to take."

QUESTION: What does it cost to obtain an EMT degree?

Ian: "The cost primarily depends on the school you attend. It can be approximately $1,000."

QUESTION: What has been the most challenging aspect of your job?

Ian: "The most challenging aspect is seeing certain patients and trying not to get emotionally involved in their family's decisions."

QUESTION: What is the most rewarding aspect of your job?

Ian: "The most rewarding part of this job is knowing that we are able to help the patients and their families in their most desperate time of need—whether it is simply transporting them to a *dialysis* appointment, transporting them home after they've been in the hospital for an extended period of time, or transporting them to the hospital in an emergency."

It takes additional tests, as well as two to five years of experience as an EMT, to become a certified flight paramedic.

QUESTION: What would you say to a young adult considering EMT as a career?

Ian: "If you are dedicated, then definitely become an EMT. It is a very rewarding career."

QUESTION: What kind of personal traits do you think are important for a EMT to have?

Ian: "To be a successful EMT, you must be able to manage your time, be organized, be able to multitask, and be able to change what you're doing at the drop of a dime."

QUESTION: Is this job what you expected when you first made the decision to get into this field?

Ian: "When I was deciding whether to go into this field, I heard what to expect from firefighter-paramedics and it has proven to be exactly what they told me it would be like."

QUESTION: Are there certain specialties within the EMT profession that are most in need today, and therefore have the greatest job opportunities and possibly job security?

Ian: "All EMTs are licensed the same. They do not have different specialties so the job market is the same. Hospital, fire department, and private agencies all hire EMTs, but they may do slightly different things, depending on protocols."

QUESTION: What kind of income can an EMT expect to make starting out? Similarly, what does an established EMT typically make?

Ian: "An EMT just starting out in a hospital or private agency will make just over minimum wage. When working in a fire department, you will be paid more because you have the fire certification and you're working for a city or a county."

 Text-Dependent Questions

1. What are two types of EMT certification courses?
2. How many calls are does the 911 emergency number receive each year in the United States?

 Research Project

Research if you would consider becoming an EMT. Write a list of pros and cons of the career and see if it is a good fit for you.

Series Glossary

accredited—a college or university program that has met all of the requirements put forth by the national organization for that job. The official stamp of approval for a degree.

Allied Health Professions—a group of professionals who use scientific principles to evaluate, diagnose and treat a variety of diseases. They also promote overall wellness and disease prevention in support of a variety of health care settings. (These may include physical therapists, dental hygienists, athletic trainers, audiologists, etc.)

American Medical Association (AMA)—the AMA is a professional group of physicians that publishes research about different areas of medicine. The AMA also advocates for its members to define medical concepts, professions, and recommendations.

anatomy—the study of the structure of living things; a person and/or animal's body.

associate's degree—a degree that is awarded to a student who has completed two years of study at a junior college, college, or university.

bachelor's degree—a degree that is awarded to a student by a college or university, usually after four years of study.

biology—the life processes especially of an organism or group.

chemistry—a science that deals with the composition, structure, and properties of substances and with the transformations that they undergo.

cardiology—the study of the heart and its action and diseases.

cardiopulmonary resuscitation (CPR)—a procedure designed to restore normal breathing after cardiac arrest that includes the clearance of air passages to the lungs, mouth-to-mouth method of artificial respiration, and heart massage by the exertion of pressure on the chest.

Centers for Disease Control—the Centers for Disease Control and Prevention (CDC) is a federal agency that conducts and supports health promotion, prevention and preparedness activities in the United States with the goal of improving overall public health.

diagnosis—to determine what is wrong with a patient. This process is especially important because it will determine the type of treatment the patient receives.

diagnostic testing—any tests performed to help determine a medical diagnosis.

EKG machine—an electrocardiogram (EKG or ECG) is a test that checks for problems with the electrical activity of your heart. An EKG shows the heart's electrical activity as line tracings on paper. The spikes and dips in the tracings are called waves. The heart is a muscular pump made up of four chambers.

first responder—the initial personnel who rush to the scene of an accident or an emergency.

Health Insurance Portability and Accountability Act (HIPAA)—a federal law enacted in 1996 that protects continuity of health coverage when a person changes or loses a job, that limits health-plan exclusions for preexisting medical conditions, that requires that patient medical information be kept private and secure, that standardizes electronic transactions involving health information, and that permits tax deduction of health insurance premiums by the self-employed.

internship—the position of a student or trainee who works in an organization, sometimes without pay, in order to gain work experience or satisfy requirements for a qualification.

kinesiology—the study of the principles of mechanics and anatomy in relation to human movement.

Master of Science degree—a Master of Science is a master's degree in the field of science awarded by universities in many countries, or a person holding such a degree.

obesity—a condition characterized by the excessive accumulation and storage of fat in the body.

pediatrics—the branch of medicine dealing with children.

physiology—a branch of biology that deals with the functions and activities of life or of living matter (as organs, tissues, or cells) and of the physical and chemical phenomena involved.

Surgeon General—the operational head of the US Public Health Department and the leading spokesperson for matters of public health.

Further Reading

Canning, Peter. *Paramedic: On the Front Lines of Medicine*.
New York: Ivy Books, an imprint of Random House
Publishing, 1997.

———. *Rescue 471: A Paramedic's Stories*. New York:
Random House Publishing Group, 2000.

Morse, Michael. *Rescuing Providence*. Boulder, CO: Paladin
Press, 2007.

Internet Resources

www.nremt.org/rwd/public/document/emt
The National Registry of Emergency Medical Technicians is a national organization that implements and regulates standards for EMTs in the United States.

www.bls.gov/ooh/healthcare/emts-and-paramedics.htm
The US Bureau of Labor Statistics is the agency that measures labor market activity, data, and working conditions in the United States.

www.cpc.mednet.ucla.edu/node/27
Information about the EMT and paramedic programs at the University of California-Los Angeles.

Index

Numbers in **bold italic** refer to captions.

About the Author

Samantha Simon has spent her career in healthcare: shadowing medical professionals, working in medical research, and as a patient liaison advocate within the industry. Her work authoring and writing about her experiences, and further studies into various aspects of the healthcare profession, has gained her unique insight into various aspects of the careers in the field of healthcare. Samantha received her Bachelor's Degree in Health Sciences Pre- Clinical Studies at the University of Central Florida. She has written and studied extensively in Neurobiology, Microbiology, Physiology, and Epidemiology, as well as worked on Medical Self-Assessment, Health Laws and Ethics, and Research Methods. She enjoys authoring and mentoring and lives in South Florida with her family and friends.